Highlights

1 FIRST GRADE
AGES 6–7

Subtraction
Learning Fun Workbook

For information about permission to reproduce selections from this bo
an entire school or school district, please contact permissions@highligh

Published by Highlights Learning • 815 Church Street • Honesdale, Pennsylv
ISBN: 978-1-68437-927-9
Mfg. 06/2020
Printed in Brainerd, MN, USA
First edition
10 9 8 7 6 5 4

D1088772

For assistance in the preparation of this book, the editors would like to thank:
Kristin Ward, MS Curriculum, Instruction, and Assessment; K–5 Mathematics and Science Instructional Coach
Jump Start Press, Inc.

Cookout Cross-Out

Mmmm . . . s'mores! Join the campers and solve these problems. Cross off to subtract. We did the first one to get you started.

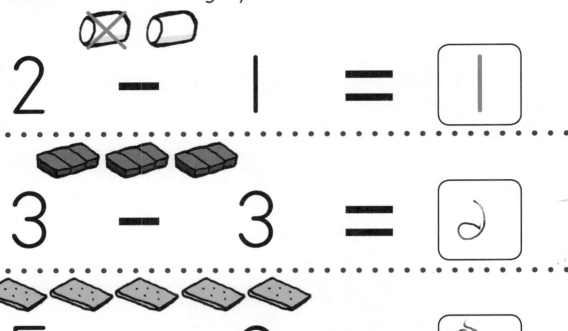

$$2 - 1 = \boxed{1}$$

$$3 - 3 = \boxed{0}$$

$$5 - 3 = \boxed{8}$$

Can you count 15 marshmallows at this cookout?

$7 - 3 = \boxed{10}$

$10 - 1 = \boxed{}$

$16 - 9 = \boxed{}$

$19 - 8 = \boxed{}$

$17 - 2 = \boxed{}$

But they call this a *pup* tent!

Hop Up and Down!

You can use a number line to subtract. Start with the first number. Then count back to the second number to find the difference.

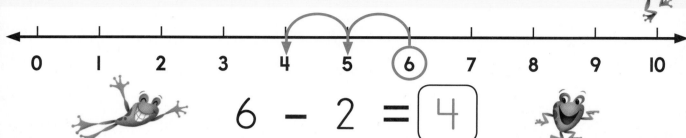

$$6 - 2 = \boxed{4}$$

You can also count up on a number line to subtract. Start with the number to subtract. Then count up to the number you subtract from to find the difference.

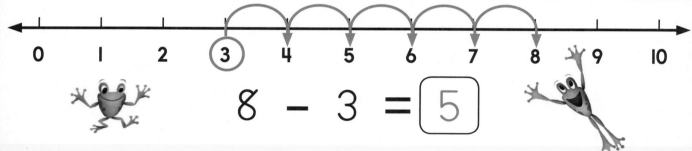

$$8 - 3 = \boxed{5}$$

Solve these subtraction problems. Count back or count up on the number line.

$$5 - 4 = \boxed{}$$ $$1 - 1 = \boxed{}$$

$$7 - 4 = \boxed{}$$ $$8 - 2 = \boxed{}$$

$$7 - 5 = \boxed{}$$ $$6 - 5 = \boxed{}$$

$$9 - 3 = \boxed{}$$ $$9 - 4 = \boxed{}$$

$$10 - 2 = \boxed{}$$ $$10 - 8 = \boxed{}$$

0 1 2 3 4 5 6 7 8 9 10 11 12 13 14 15 16 17 18 19 20

14 − 1 = ☐   12 − 8 = ☐

17 − 9 = ☐   15 − 5 = ☐

11 − 5 = ☐   19 − 2 = ☐

Each frog has an exact match. Draw lines between the matching pairs.

Candy Counter

You can draw and count to subtract. Here's how.

14 − 5 = ?
Draw 14 circles.
Cross off 5 of the circles.
Count the remaining circles.
You have 9 circles left,
So . . .
14 − 5 = 9

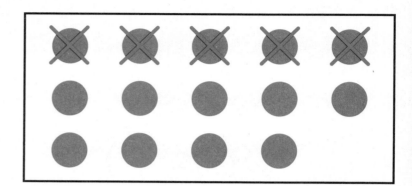

Count to solve the subtraction problems on these two pages. Draw gumdrops, gumballs, lollipops, or just circles to show your thinking.

7 − 5 = ☐

6 − 3 = ☐

8 − 1 = ☐

5 − 2 = ☐

4 − 3 = ☐

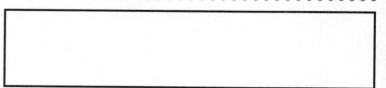

What candy is never on time for school?
Choco-late.

12 − 1 = ☐

15 − 6 = ☐

11 − 2 = ☐

14 − 8 = ☐

13 − 5 = ☐

Count the lollipops on the candy counter. After someone buys all the yellow lollipops, how many lollipops are left?

 ☐ − ☐ = ☐

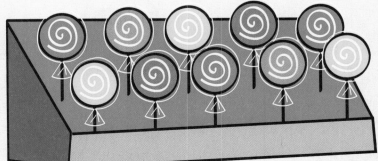

Bowling Frames

You can use **10-frames** to show a subtraction problem. Here's how.

12 − 7 = ?
First show 12 circles in the 10-frames.
Cross off 7 circles.
Count the remaining circles.
You have 5 circles left.
So . . .
12 − 7 = 5

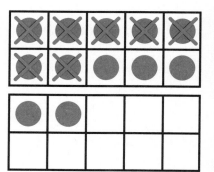

Draw circles in 10-frames to show each problem. Then complete the subtraction problem.

9 − 4 =

8 − 2 =

7 − 3 =

9 − 6 =

8 − 5 =

Operations and Algebraic Thinking: Subtraction Strategies Within 20

13 − 11 = ☐

16 − 10 = ☐

15 − 8 = ☐

17 − 9 = ☐

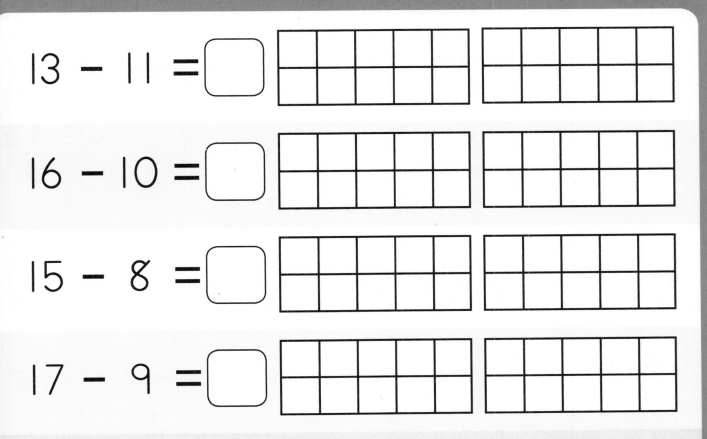

Strike! Someone knocked down all **10** pins in this frame. Follow the lines to find out who.

What Belongs?

You can use a **number bond** to take apart a problem. It shows how 2 parts (smaller numbers) add up to make a whole (larger number). More than I pair of numbers might work with the same larger number.

Here's what those might look like. Paul has **9** rubber balls. Some are big and some are small. How many of each size could he have?

Taking apart **a whole** is another way to think about subtraction.

· ·

Take apart a subtraction problem using a number bond. Then solve the problem. We did one to get you started.

15 − 10 = [5]

15 − 9 = [ ]

15 − 7 = [ ]

15 − 3 = [ ]

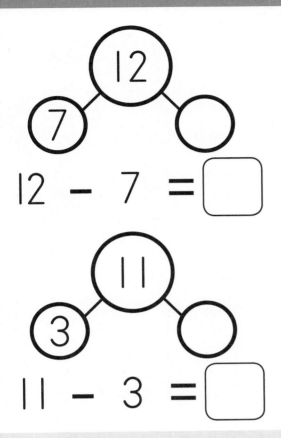

12

7

$12 - 7 = \boxed{}$

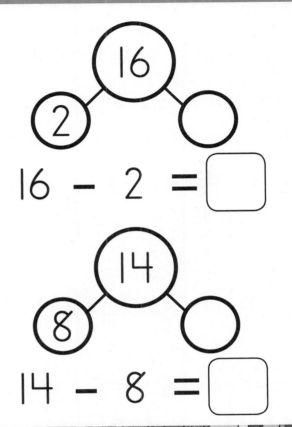

16

2

$16 - 2 = \boxed{}$

11

3

$11 - 3 = \boxed{}$

14

8

$14 - 8 = \boxed{}$

Circle the **8** objects in this Hidden Pictures puzzle. Can you also see which toys belong in which boxes?

scissors

wristwatch

ring

sock

pencil

apple

horseshoe

bread

Fact Family Homes

You can use **fact families** to help solve subtraction and addition problems. Write in the numbers to complete each family. We did the first one to get you started.

A fact family **is** a group of math facts that use the same numbers.

House 1

7
4   3

$4 + 3 = \boxed{7}$

$\boxed{3} + 4 = 7$

$7 - \boxed{4} = 3$

$\boxed{7} - 3 = 4$

House 2

9
2   11

$9 + 2 = \boxed{}$

$\boxed{} + 9 = 11$

$11 - \boxed{} = 2$

$\boxed{} - 2 = 9$

House 3

9
6   3

$6 + \boxed{} = 9$

$\boxed{} + 6 = 9$

$\boxed{} - 6 = 3$

$9 - 3 = \boxed{}$

House 4

12
5   7

$5 + 7 = \boxed{}$

$\boxed{} + 5 = 12$

$12 - \boxed{} = 7$

$\boxed{} - 7 = 5$

House 1 (8, 7, 1)

$7 + \boxed{} = \boxed{}$

$\boxed{} + 7 = \boxed{}$

$8 - 7 = \boxed{}$

$\boxed{} - \boxed{} = 7$

House 2 (20, 15, 5)

$5 + 15 = \boxed{}$

$\boxed{} + 5 = 20$

$20 - \boxed{} = \boxed{}$

$\boxed{} - 15 = 5$

House 3 (14, 12, 2)

$12 + 2 = \boxed{}$

$\boxed{} + 12 = 14$

$\boxed{} - 2 = 12$

$14 - \boxed{} = 2$

House 4 (13, 10, 3)

$\boxed{} + \boxed{} = \boxed{}$

$\boxed{} + \boxed{} = \boxed{}$

$\boxed{} - \boxed{} = \boxed{}$

$\boxed{} - \boxed{} = \boxed{}$

Knock, knock.
Who's there?
Justin.
Justin who?
Justin the neighborhood. I thought I'd drop by.

Slide Ride

You can use an addition fact to subtract. A number bond can help, too. Here's how.

14 − 5 = [?]

Slide out the 5 and think:

5 + [?] = 14

You know that 5 and 9 adds up to 14.

5 + [9] = 14

So . . .

14 − 5 = [9]

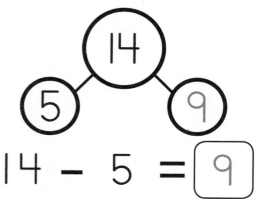

14 − 5 = [9]

• •

Solve each subtraction problem by using an addition fact. We did the first one to get you started.

5 − 3 = [2]

3 + [2] = 5

7 − 3 = [ ]

4 + [ ] = 7

Connect the dots from 1 to 20 to see some sliding fun!

Operations and Algebraic Thinking: Subtraction Strategies Within 20

19 − 1 = ☐

1 + ☐ = 19

11 − 10 = ☐

10 + ☐ = 11

14 − 4 = ☐

4 + ☐ = 14

17 − 5 = ☐

5 + ☐ = 17

Sasha is putting coats on her dogs. Look at the number pattern. Can you figure out what number coat the last dog should wear? You can use addition or subtraction to figure it out.

☐

13 − 2 = ☐

2 + ☐ = 13

10 − 5 = ☐

5 + ☐ = 10

15

Make a Switch

Switch the numbers so that a subtraction problem becomes an addition problem. Then choose an addition strategy. We did the first one to get you started.

$6 - 5 = \boxed{1}$

$\boxed{1} + 5 = 6$

$8 - 3 = \boxed{}$

$\boxed{} + 3 = 8$

$7 - 5 = \boxed{}$

$\boxed{} + 5 = 7$

$17 - 9 = \boxed{}$

$\boxed{} + 9 = 17$

$12 - 6 = \boxed{}$

$\boxed{} + 6 = 12$

$9 - 5 = \boxed{}$

$\boxed{} + 5 = 9$

Each of these silly picture pairs rhymes. But 2 of the animals are in the wrong spot! Which 2 should switch places?

$$19 - 9 = \boxed{}$$

$$\boxed{} + 9 = 19$$

You can use your fingers to help you add or subtract.

$$11 - 4 = \boxed{}$$

$$\boxed{} + 4 = 11$$

$$20 - 11 = \boxed{}$$

$$\boxed{} + 11 = 20$$

$$15 - 12 = \boxed{}$$

$$\boxed{} + 12 = 15$$

$$13 - 2 = \boxed{}$$

$$\boxed{} + 2 = 13$$

$$10 - 8 = \boxed{}$$

$$\boxed{} + 8 = 10$$

$$12 - 7 = \boxed{}$$

$$\boxed{} + 7 = 12$$

Subtraction works for words, too! For example, **CROW − R = COW**. Take away letters from each of these animal names to find a different animal.

Subtract 1 letter:
1. FOX
2. BEAGLE

Subtract 2 letters:
3. HYENA
4. BEAVER

Subtract 3 letters:
5. RABBIT

Fall Harvest

Pick your own apples and pumpkins! Draw to show how to solve each take-from word problem. Then finish the equation. We did one to get you started.

Tomika has **9 red apples**🍎. She gives some to Ty. If Tomika has **4 red apples** 🍎 left, how many did she give to Ty?

One way to think about subtraction is to take a part away from a whole. You can use take-from to find a missing number.

● ● ● ● ✖
✖ ✖ ✖ ✖

$$9 - \boxed{5} = 4$$

Eric has some green apples. He gives **4 green apples** 🍏 to Sasha. If Eric has **7 green apples** 🍏 left, how many apples did he have to start?

$$\boxed{} - 4 = 7$$

One tree has **19 yellow apples** 🍎. If Grandpa picks **15 yellow apples** 🍎 from the tree, how many yellow apples are left on the tree?

$$19 - 15 = \boxed{}$$

Jenna finds **12 pumpkins** in the field. She picks **4** of the **pumpkins**. How many pumpkins are left in the field?

$$12 - 4 = \boxed{}$$

The farmer has **20 pieces of candy**. She gives **1** piece to every child who visits her farm. Now she has **3 pieces of candy** left. How many pieces of candy did she give away?

$$20 - \boxed{} = 3$$

What silly things do you see at the farm?

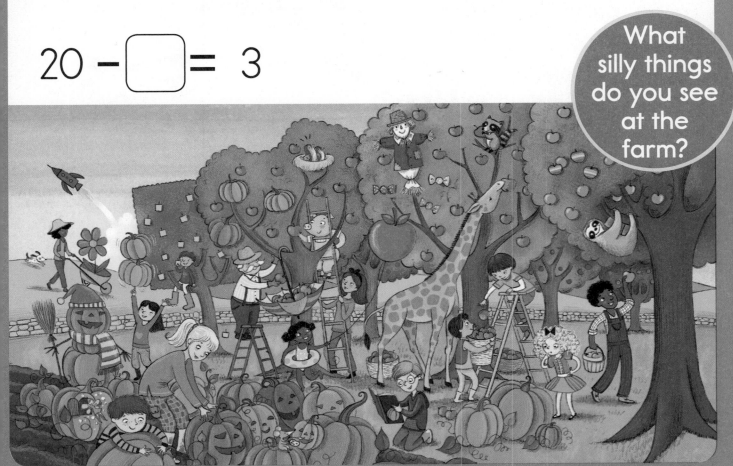

19

True Route

When you subtract, the order of the numbers is important. If you change the order, the difference will not be the same.

$8 - 3 = 3 - 8$ is **false** because $8 - 3 = 5$ but $3 - 8$ does not equal 5.

$8 + 3 = 3 + 8$ is **true** because $8 + 3 = 11$ and $3 + 8 = 11$.

Help Logan get to his cabin without getting his feet wet. Circle each equation that is true. Then draw a line from the true logs to his cabin.

FINISH

$3+6=6+3$

$11-11=11-11$

$9-8=8-9$

$8+9=9+8$

$7-2=2-7$

$13-3=3-13$

$12+1=1+12$

$4+14=4+14$

$9+1=1+9$

$10+5=5+10$

START

$0-2=2-0$

$4-18=18-4$

Let's Balance!

An equation is **true**, or equal, if the difference is the same on both sides of the equal sign. An equation is **false**, or not equal, if a difference on one side of the equal sign is more or less than the other difference.

$$7 - 4 = 9 - 6$$

$$3 = 3 \quad \text{TRUE}$$

$$7 - 4 = 9 - 5$$

$$3 = 4 \quad \text{FALSE}$$

Help balance each scale! Fill in the missing numbers on the scales below to make each equation true. We did one to get you started.

$$7 - 5 = 18 - \boxed{16}$$

$$10 - 2 = \boxed{} - 1$$

$$12 - \boxed{} = 9 - 0$$

$$\boxed{} - 4 = 10 - 2$$

$$20 - 7 = 18 - \boxed{}$$

$$14 - 1 = 16 - \boxed{}$$

Who's Related?

You can use the same numbers to show addition and subtraction facts that are related. Here's what that looks like:

$12 - 5 = 7$ and $5 + 7 = 12$ are related

$10 + 4 = 14$ and $10 - 4 = 6$ are not related

Solve each problem. See which problems are part of the same fact family. Then draw a line between each pair of equations that are related. We did the first one to get you started.

$13 - 7 = \boxed{6}$

$5 + 7 = \boxed{}$

$11 - 3 = \boxed{}$

$8 + 5 = \boxed{}$

$9 + 3 = \boxed{}$

$15 - 3 = \boxed{}$

$12 - 7 = \boxed{}$

$3 + 8 = \boxed{}$

$6 + 7 = \boxed{13}$

$15 - 12 = \boxed{}$

$13 - 5 = \boxed{}$

$12 - 9 = \boxed{}$

Operations and Algebraic Thinking: Addition/Subtraction Relationship

Solve each problem. Then draw a line between each pair of equations that are related.

6 + 8 = ☐   6 + 12 = ☐

12 − 5 = ☐   13 − 6 = ☐

18 − 6 = ☐   14 − 6 = ☐

7 + 6 = ☐   7 + 5 = ☐

Find and circle the **5** objects in this Hidden Pictures puzzle. What do the objects have in common?

lizard   ladder

ladybug

letter
lamp

Check It Out

Fact families **can** help you see if your subtraction is correct.

You can check subtraction by using addition. Here's how.

Start with 7. Take away 4. $7 - 4 = ?$

There are 3 left. $7 - 4 = 3$

Then add 3 and 4 back together. $3 + 4 = 7$ ✓

Ready to be a checker? Solve the subtraction problem. Then turn it into an addition problem. Does your answer check out? Check the box! We did one to get you started.

$$7 - 2 = \boxed{5}$$
$$\boxed{5} + \boxed{2} = \boxed{7} \;\checkmark$$

$$8 - 5 = \boxed{}$$
$$\boxed{} + \boxed{} = \boxed{} \;\square$$

$$4 - 1 = \boxed{}$$
$$\boxed{} + \boxed{} = \boxed{} \;\square$$

$$10 - 3 = \boxed{}$$
$$\boxed{} + \boxed{} = \boxed{} \;\square$$

$$9 - 7 = \boxed{}$$
$$\boxed{} + \boxed{} = \boxed{} \;\square$$

$$7 - 6 = \boxed{}$$
$$\boxed{} + \boxed{} = \boxed{} \;\square$$

Find the **2** checkerboards that are the same. How many checkers does each board have? Which board has the fewest checkers?

Operations and Algebraic Thinking: Addition/Subtraction Relationship

17 − 2 = ☐

☐ + ☐ = ☐ ☐

11 − 4 = ☐

☐ + ☐ = ☐ ☐

19 − 16 = ☐

☐ + ☐ = ☐ ☐

18 − 8 = ☐

☐ + ☐ = ☐ ☐

12 − 1 = ☐

☐ + ☐ = ☐ ☐

14 − 9 = ☐

☐ + ☐ = ☐ ☐

Double check this game of checkers. Can you check off **21** differences between these pictures?

Lost in the Laundry

A number is lost in each of these addition problems! Show the subtraction that helps you solve the problem. You might use a number bond to help. We did the first one to get you started.

$6 + 2 = 8$

$8 - 6 = 2$

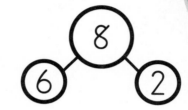

$\boxed{} + 3 = 11$

$\boxed{} - \boxed{} = \boxed{}$

$8 + \boxed{} = 15$

$\boxed{} - \boxed{} = \boxed{}$

$7 + \boxed{} = 13$

$\boxed{} - \boxed{} = \boxed{}$

$\boxed{} + 6 = 10$

$\boxed{} - \boxed{} = \boxed{}$

$\boxed{} + 3 = 12$

$\boxed{} - \boxed{} = \boxed{}$

What does a lost sock look for?

Its sole mate.

Operations and Algebraic Thinking: Addition/Subtraction Relationship

☐ + 7 = 9   ☐ + 2 = 12
☐ − ☐ = ☐   ☐ − ☐ = ☐

☐ + 5 = 14   8 + ☐ = 16
☐ − ☐ = ☐   ☐ − ☐ = ☐

Can you find **20** missing socks in this laundromat? We found one to get you started.

Dive-In Movie

You can use the different subtraction strategies to solve word problems.

It's showtime! Write a subtraction equation to solve each word problem. Show your thinking. You can draw circles to represent the items, use a number line, or use 10-frames.

Ollie octopus bought **8 tickets** to the movies. He gave **6 tickets** to his friends. How many tickets did Ollie have left?

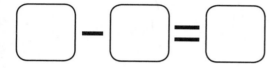

There were **12 seahorses** at the first show. Then **4 seahorses** swam away before the second show. How many seahorses stayed?

Say this tongue twister three times fast:

Four flat fish slap fins.

Yesterday **20 fish** bought tickets to the movies. Today only **13 fish** bought tickets. How many fewer fish were there today?

☐ − ☐ = ☐

There were **16 lobsters** and **7 crabs** at the show. How many more lobsters than crabs were there?

☐ − ☐ = ☐

Something's fishy! What silly things do you see under the sea?

Art Parts

Everyone is getting ready for the school arts and crafts show. Can you help them gather their supplies? Draw a picture to help you solve each problem. Then write the equation to solve each word problem.

Pennies or buttons are also good tools to help solve problems.

Martin has **2 fewer paintbrushes** than Annie. Annie has **5 paintbrushes**. How many paintbrushes does Martin have?

Ava has **9 markers**. She has **3 more markers** than David. How many markers does David have?

Quincy shares all her crayons with Beth and Casey. She gives Beth **4 more crayons** than she gives to Casey. Beth has **8 crayons**. How many crayons does Casey have?

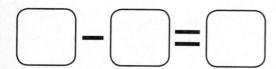

Tariq has **20 stickers** ⭐. Lia has **4 fewer stickers** ⭐ than Tariq. How many stickers does Lia have?

☐ – ☐ = ☐

Bailey needs **15 blue beads** ● to finish her necklace. She only has **6 blue beads** ●. How many **more** beads does she need?

☐ – ☐ = ☐

What silly things do you see at the art show?

31

Sandy's Strategy

Sandy's favorite number is 10. Why? Finding 10 makes subtraction easier. Sandy uses a subtraction strategy called **decomposing**, or breaking apart, numbers to use a 10 to subtract.

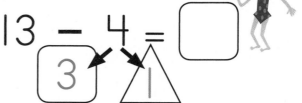

STEP 1:
I know that 13 – 3 will be 10.
So I break apart 4 into 3 and 1.

$$13 - 4 = \square$$
$$\boxed{3} \quad \triangle 1$$

STEP 2:
Next I subtract 3 from 13 to find 10.

$$13 - \boxed{3} = 10$$

STEP 3:
Then I subtract 1 from 10 to get 9.

$$10 - \triangle 1 = \boxed{9}$$

So . . .
The difference between 13 and 4 is 9.

$$13 - 4 = \boxed{9}$$

Use Sandy's strategy to solve the subtraction problems on these two pages.

$$16 - 7 = \square$$
$$\square \quad \triangle$$

$$16 - \square = 10$$

$$10 - \triangle = \square$$

So . . .
$$16 - 7 = \square$$

$$14 - 5 = \square$$
$$\square \quad \triangle$$

$$14 - \square = 10$$

$$10 - \triangle = \square$$

So . . .
$$14 - 5 = \square$$

17 − 9 = ☐

☐ △

17 − ☐ = 10

10 − △ = ☐

So . . .
17 − 9 = ☐

15 − 8 = ☐

☐ △

15 − ☐ = 10

10 − △ = ☐

So . . .
15 − 8 = ☐

Which **3** pieces will finish the puzzle? Draw lines to place each piece.

Have a Ball!

You can count back by tens or draw pictures to subtract tens. Draw to show how you solve the problem. You might use 10-frames or a number line.

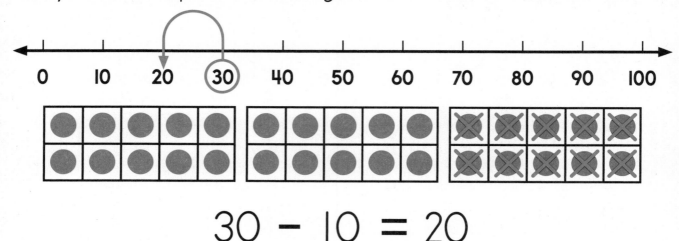

$$30 - 10 = 20$$

$10 - 10 = \boxed{}$

$80 - 50 = \boxed{}$

$40 - 20 = \boxed{}$

$70 - 10 = \boxed{}$

$90 - 10 = \boxed{}$

$70 - 30 = \boxed{}$

$70 - 20 = \boxed{}$

$100 - 20 = \boxed{}$

50 − 10 = ☐   80 − 30 = ☐

40 − 30 = ☐   10 − 0 = ☐

60 − 30 = ☐   90 − 30 = ☐

Find and circle **10** balls at the playground. Color in a ball as you find each one.

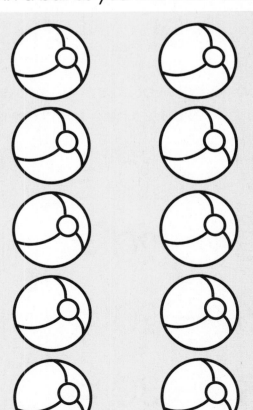

Silly Sheep

You can use a hundred chart to subtract tens. You can also use a hundred chart to subtract a one-digit number from a two-digit number. Here's how.

$51 - 30 =$?

To subtract tens, start on 51. Count back three 10s. So . . .

$51 - 30 =$ 21

$17 - 5 =$?

Start at 17. Move left and count back 5. So . . .

$17 - 5 =$ 12

1	2	3	4	5	6	7	8	9	10
11	12	13	14	15	16	17	18	19	20
21	22	23	24	25	26	27	28	29	30
31	32	33	34	35	36	37	38	39	40
41	42	43	44	45	46	47	48	49	50
51	52	53	54	55	56	57	58	59	60
61	62	63	64	65	66	67	68	69	70
71	72	73	74	75	76	77	78	79	80
81	82	83	84	85	86	87	88	89	90
91	92	93	94	95	96	97	98	99	100

Solve each problem on these two pages using the hundred chart. Then use the letters next to the answers to solve the riddle on the next page.

$73 - 10 =$ ☐ D $27 - 20 =$ ☐ K

$54 - 20 =$ ☐ E $55 - 40 =$ ☐ O

$68 - 20 =$ ☐ H $91 - 30 =$ ☐ W

$83 - 30 =$ ☐ I $32 - 20 =$ ☐ N

11 − 9 = ☐ E   17 − 3 = ☐ S

14 − 8 = ☐ O   18 − 9 = ☐ T

12 − 7 = ☐ P   13 − 5 = ☐ W

19 − 8 = ☐ R   20 − 4 = ☐ Z

How many sheep does it take to knit a sweater?

___ ___ ___ ___ . ___ ___ ___ ___ ___
16 34 11 15   14 48 34   2   5

,

___ ___ ___ ___   ___ ___ ___ ___
63   6 12   9   7 12   6   8

___ ___ ___ ___   ___ ___
48 15 61   9   6

___ ___ ___ ___ !
 7 12 53   9

Tower Power!

You can draw or build to show a problem subtracting tens from a two-digit number. You can also draw or build to show subtracting a one-digit number from a two-digit number. Cross off cubes below each problem to help you find the answer. We did the first two to get you started.

88 − 10 = [78]

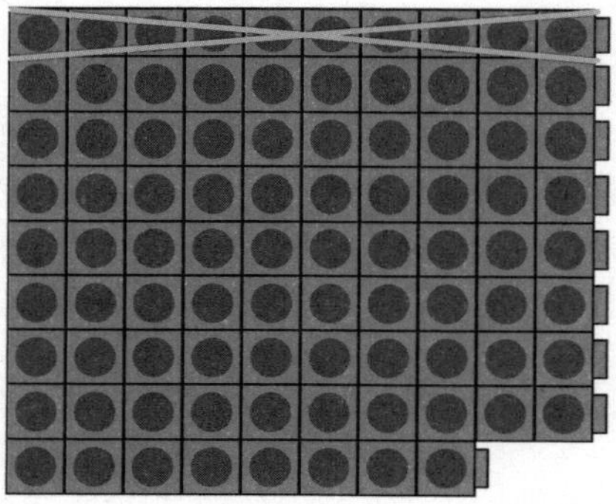

17 − 1 = [16]

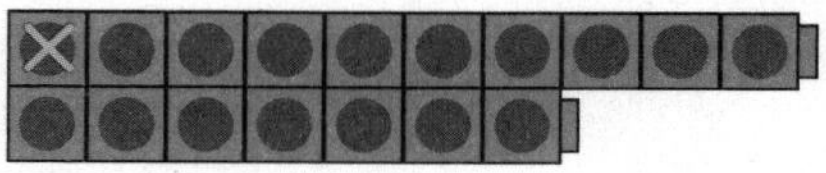

14 − 2 = [ ]

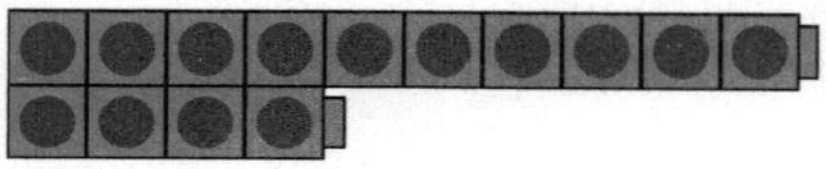

20 − 3 = [ ]

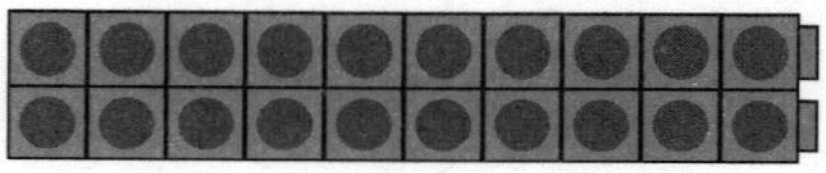

38 − 20 = [ ]

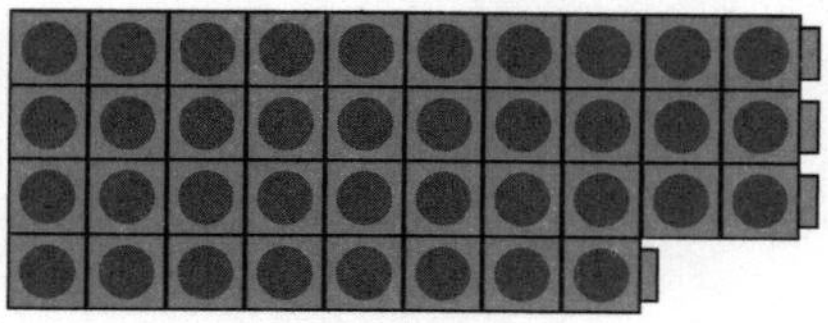

16 − 7 = [ ]

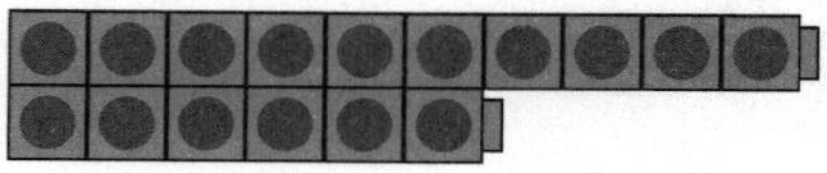

$15 - 7 = \boxed{}$

$12 - 8 = \boxed{}$

$68 - 20 = \boxed{}$

$53 - 10 = \boxed{}$

Which tower uses the most blocks? What is the difference in the number of blocks between the tallest tower and the shortest tower?

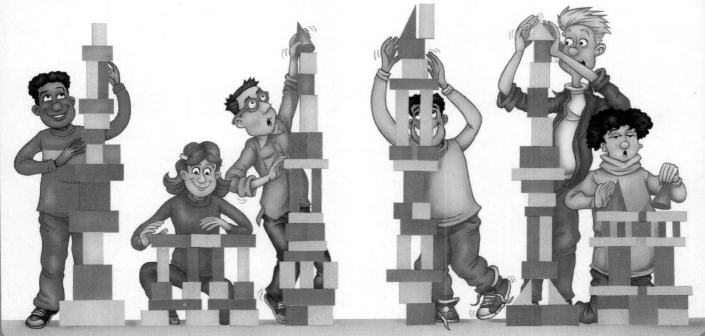

Above and Below

Use your head to find **10 less** and **10 more**. We did the first one for you.

10 LESS		10 MORE
39	49	59
	63	
	14	
	49	

10 LESS		10 MORE
	25	
	57	
	30	
	88	

You can use mental math to count on or back by tens.

Use blue to color each space that has a number you wrote in the chart. You'll see something that's over your head!

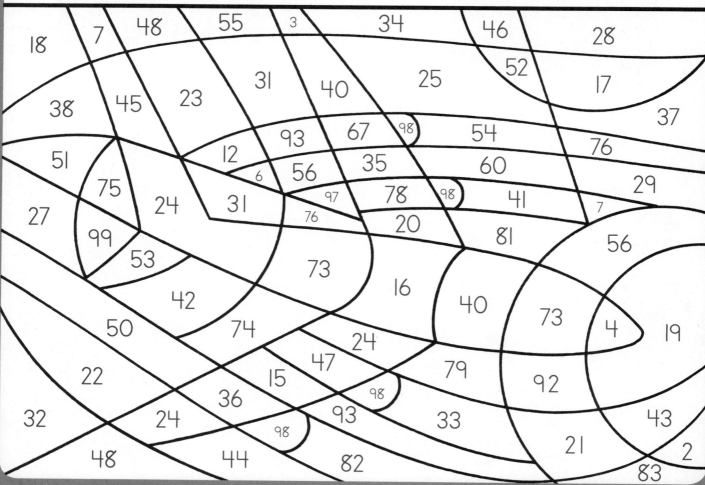

Now start with **10 more**.

10 MORE		10 LESS		10 MORE		10 LESS
66	56				32	
	71				85	
	90				47	
	11				10	

Color each space that has a number you wrote in the chart. Color the **10-more** spaces **red**. Color the **10-less** spaces **orange**. You'll see something that uses your feet!

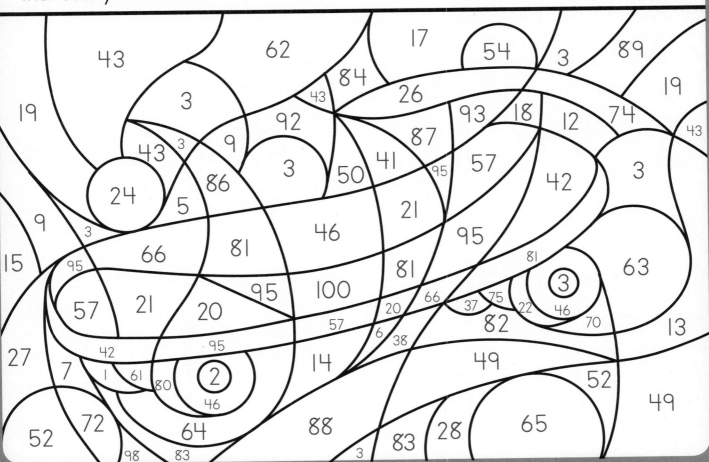

You'll Love This!

Use a hundred chart to subtract **2 two-digit** numbers. For each **ten** you subtract, move up 1 row. Solve the equations on both pages. Color a box in the chart for each answer you find and you'll see a lovely shape. We did the first to get you started.

1	2	3	4	5	6	7	8	9	10
11	12	13	14	15	16	17	18	19	20
21	22	23	24	25	26	27	28	29	30
31	32	33	34	35	36	37	38	39	40
41	42	43	44	45	46	47	48	49	50
51	52	53	54	55	56	57	58	59	60
61	62	63	64	65	66	67	68	69	70
71	72	73	74	75	76	77	78	79	80
81	82	83	84	85	86	87	88	89	90
91	92	93	94	95	96	97	98	99	100

$84 - 20 = \boxed{64}$

$42 - 10 = \boxed{}$

$85 - 10 = \boxed{}$

$56 - 30 = \boxed{}$

$93 - 40 = \boxed{}$

$78 - 60 = \boxed{}$

64 − 50 = ☐

79 − 30 = ☐

35 − 10 = ☐

87 − 20 = ☐

43 − 30 = ☐

59 − 20 = ☐

82 − 60 = ☐

78 − 20 = ☐

97 − 80 = ☐

86 − 10 = ☐

69 − 40 = ☐

92 − 50 = ☐

Tackle This!

It's time for the big football game! The fans in Rows A to G are here to cheer on the Dolphins 🏈 and the Roosters 🏈! Solve these word problems to find out what happened at the game. You can use any of the subtraction strategies you've learned.

Row A is packed with **18** fans. But only **4** are **Roosters fans** 🏈. How many are **Dolphins fans**?

$$\boxed{} - \boxed{} = \boxed{}$$

The total of all fans in the rows is **84**. There are **50 Roosters fans** 🏈. How many are **Dolphins fan**?

$$\boxed{} - \boxed{} = \boxed{}$$

Row B has **13 Dolphins fans** 🏈. All but **5** of those fans were wearing **blue hats** 🧢. How many are wearing **blue hats**?

$$\boxed{} - \boxed{} = \boxed{}$$

Row C has **16 Roosters fans** 🏈, and **13** of them are wearing **orange scarves** 🧣. How many are not wearing **orange scarves**?

$$\boxed{} - \boxed{} = \boxed{}$$

Pete brings **17 bags of peanuts** to sell. At the end of the day, he has **2 bags left**. How many **bags of peanuts** did Pete sell?

☐ − ☐ = ☐

There are **19 people** in Row G. During halftime, **11 people** go to the snack bar. How many **people** are left in Row G?

☐ − ☐ = ☐

The Dolphins score **42 points** to win! They scored **20 points** in the first half of the game. How many **points** did they score in the second half?

☐ − ☐ = ☐

Can you spot at least **20** differences between these pictures?

1 FIRST GRADE

Congratulations!

_____
(your name)

worked hard
and finished the

Subtraction
Learning Fun Workbook

Answers

Inside Front Cover

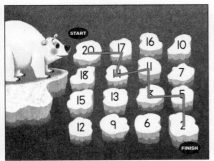

Pages 2–3
Cookout Cross-Out

2 − 1 = 1   3 − 3 = 0   5 − 3 = 2

7 − 3 = 4
10 − 1 = 9
16 − 9 = 7
19 − 8 = 11
17 − 2 = 15

Pages 4–5
Hop Up and Down!

5 − 4 = 1	1 − 1 = 0
7 − 4 = 3	8 − 2 = 6
7 − 5 = 2	6 − 5 = 1
9 − 3 = 6	9 − 4 = 5
10 − 2 = 8	10 − 8 = 2
14 − 1 = 13	12 − 8 = 4
17 − 9 = 8	15 − 5 = 10
11 − 5 = 6	19 − 2 = 17

Pages 4–5
Hop Up and Down!

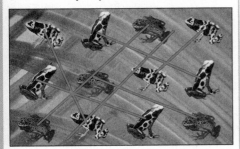

Pages 6–7
Candy Counter

7 − 5 = 2	12 − 1 = 11
6 − 3 = 3	15 − 6 = 9
8 − 1 = 7	11 − 2 = 9
5 − 2 = 3	14 − 8 = 6
4 − 3 = 1	13 − 5 = 8

$$10 - 3 = 7$$

Pages 8–9
Bowling Frames

9 − 4 = 5	9 − 6 = 3	16 − 10 = 6
8 − 2 = 6	8 − 5 = 3	15 − 8 = 7
7 − 3 = 4	13 − 11 = 2	17 − 9 = 8

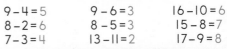

Pages 10–11
What Belongs?

15 − 10 = 5
15 − 7 = 8
15 − 9 = 6
15 − 3 = 12

12 − 7 = 5
11 − 3 = 8
16 − 2 = 14
14 − 8 = 6

Pages 12–13
Fact Family Homes

4 7 3
4 + 3 = 7
3 + 4 = 7
7 − 4 = 3
7 − 3 = 4

6 9 3
6 + 3 = 9
3 + 6 = 9
9 − 6 = 3
9 − 3 = 6

2 9 11
9 + 2 = 11
2 + 9 = 11
11 − 9 = 2
11 − 2 = 9

5 12 7
5 + 7 = 12
7 + 5 = 12
12 − 5 = 7
12 − 7 = 5

7 8 1
7 + 1 = 8
1 + 7 = 8
8 − 7 = 1
8 − 1 = 7

15 20 5
5 + 15 = 20
15 + 5 = 20
20 − 5 = 15
20 − 15 = 5

12 14 2
12 + 2 = 14
2 + 12 = 14
14 − 2 = 12
14 − 12 = 2

10 13 3
3 + 10 = 13
10 + 3 = 13
13 − 3 = 10
13 − 10 = 3

Pages 14–15
Slide Ride

5 − 3 = 2	19 − 1 = 18	13 − 2 = 11
3 + 2 = 5	1 + 18 = 19	2 + 11 = 13
7 − 3 = 4	14 − 4 = 10	10 − 5 = 5
4 + 3 = 7	4 + 10 = 14	5 + 5 = 10
The last dog should wear number 15	17 − 5 = 12	11 − 10 = 1
	5 + 12 = 17	10 + 1 = 11

Pages 16–17
Make a Switch

DUCK/BOX should switch with FOX/TRUCK

Answers

Pages 16–17
Make a Switch

$6-5=1$
$1+5=6$
$7-5=2$
$2+5=7$
$12-6=6$
$6+6=12$

$8-3=5$
$5+3=8$
$17-9=8$
$8+9=17$
$9-5=4$
$4+5=9$

$19-9=10$
$10+9=19$
$11-4=7$
$7+4=11$
$15-12=3$
$3+12=15$

$10-8=2$
$2+8=10$
$20-11=9$
$9+11=20$
$13-2=11$
$11+2=13$
$12-7=5$
$5+7=12$

Subtract 1 letter:
1. FOX OX
2. BEAGLE EAGLE

Subtract 2 letters:
3. HYENA HEN
4. BEAVER BEAR

Subtract 3 letters:
5. RABBIT RAT

Pages 18–19
Fall Harvest

$9-5=4$ $12-4=8$
$11-4=7$ $20-17=3$
$19-15=4$

Page 20
True Route

Pages 22–23
Who's Related?

$13-7=6$ $12-7=5$
$5+7=12$ $3+8=11$
$11-3=8$ $6+7=13$
$8+5=13$ $15-12=3$
$9+3=12$ $13-5=8$
$15-3=12$ $12-9=3$

$6+8=14$ $6+12=18$
$12-5=7$ $13-6=7$
$18-6=12$ $14-6=8$
$7+6=13$ $7+5=12$

Page 21
Let's Balance!

$7-5=18-16$

$10-2=9-1$

$12-3=9-0$

$12-4=10-2$

$20-7=18-5$

$14-1=16-3$

Pages 24–25
Check It Out

$7-2=5$ $8-5=3$
$5+2=7$ $3+5=8$

$17-2=15$ $11-4=7$
$15+2=17$ $7+4=11$

$4-1=3$ $10-3=7$
$3+1=4$ $7+3=10$

$19-16=3$ $18-8=10$
$3+16=19$ $10+8=18$

$9-7=2$ $7-6=1$
$2+7=9$ $1+6=7$

$12-1=11$ $14-9=5$
$11+1=12$ $5+9=14$

13 13 13 13 13 12

Pages 26–27
Lost in the Laundry

$8+3=11$ $8+7=15$ $9+5=14$
$11-8=3$ $15-8=7$ $14-9=5$

$7+6=13$ $4+6=10$ $10+2=12$
$13-7=6$ $10-4=6$ $12-10=2$

$9+3=12$ $2+7=9$ $8+8=16$
$12-9=3$ $9-2=7$ $16-8=8$

Pages 28–29
Dive-In Movie

$8-6=2$ $20-13=7$
$12-4=8$ $16-7=9$

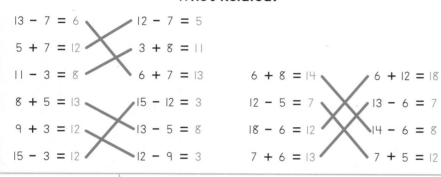